Huckleberry
Jon and Amy's Home
Amy's playhouse
Hollow
Huckleberry Creek
Huckleberry Falls
Harry Bear's fishing hole
Bucky Beaver's Dam
Eagle's Nest
den
Harry Bears Cave
Nibbles the Mouse
Moose

Huckleberry Hollow Publishing

presents
the first book in the Huckleberry Hollow Children's Book Series

Snowboarding Bunny

Text and illustrations
by Bonita Forsyth

This book is dedicated to
John Forsyth

Watercolor and acrylic paints on D'arches watercolor paper
were used for the full-color artwork.
The text type is New Roman Times.

Printed and bound in Canada by Friesens

Inquiries should be addressed to:
Huckleberry Hollow Publishing
C20 Forbes Rd, RR1, Lac la Hache, BC
Canada, V0K 1T0

ISBN 1-55056-612-1

Canadian Cataloguing in Publication Data

Forsyth, Bonita
Snowboarding bunny

(Huckleberry Hollow childrens book series; 1)
ISBN 1-55056-612-1

I. Title. II. Series
PS8561.0697S66 1998 jC813'.54 C98-910746-9
PZ7.F778Sn 1998

Snowboarding Bunny

Bonita Forsyth

One warm, sunny morning in early summer a mother snowshoe hare brought into the world her beautiful family. There was Cuddly Bunny, Clumsy Bunny, Chubby Bunny and Sunny Bunny. Sunny Bunny was named for the warm golden colours that were sprinkled through his soft brown fur. He opened his eyes for the first time in that cozy protective den to the warm golden sunlight streaming in through the cracks in the overhead log.

It was only a very short time before Sunny became aware of the marvelous strength of his hind legs. He couldn't wait to explore the forest floor that lay just outside the opening to the den!

Each day Sunny would eagerly explore the surrounding forest with his Mother, Brothers and Sisters. He would sniff and nibble at everything in his path and was delighted with the distance his long hind legs carried him.

It wasn't long before he was exploring on his own, far ahead of his family.

He was a good little hare, mindful of the dangers his mother had warned him of. He knew to hide when he saw the overhead shadow of large birds. He knew to be still when he smelled the sharp scent of prowling predators so the colours of his fur would blend in with the colours of the surrounding forest.

Sunny Bunny loved romping and playing his days away. He would leap great distances from stumps to rocks and back again.

He even dared to propel himself through the air at such speed and distance he could outsmart Wylee Fox on the chase and leave him sniffing about for hours for a clue to his whereabouts.

He was very proud of this trick!

But it was that feeling of sheer joy while leaping and twisting in the air that Sunny Bunny loved!

As the cooler weather approached and the days became shorter, Sunny Bunny began to notice some changes. Not only were the leaves and grass changing colour, so was he!

Flecks of white were showing up everywhere in his fur!

Then one misty moonlit evening cold white flakes fell from the sky. By morning the ground was covered with a soft blanket of snow. The snow continued to fall all day long while Sunny sat with his family in the den watching the forest floor disappear.

Finally the snow stopped falling and the sun came out. The freshly fallen snow sparkled in the sunlight and looked very inviting.

As Sunny ventured out into this cold unknown he was surprised to find that he was not sinking! His large furry feet kept him hopping effortlessly over the snow. But, alas, when he went to leap and jump the snow was not solid enough to give him any great height or distance!

Now he would never be able to tease Wylee Fox. And, instead of eating sweet grass and succulent plants, he had to nibble the bark and twigs that showed above the snow.

He did, however, enjoy the frozen rose hips. They were very cold but as they melted on his tongue, they filled his mouth with a bittersweet flavour he very much enjoyed.

Sunny Bunny still, however, missed the jumping and leaping activities that used to fill his sunny Autumn days.

One afternoon Sunny Bunny came across a sign he had never noticed before.

As he continued down this unfamiliar path, he was suddenly aware of the fast approaching sound of singing, laughing and whooping. He had never heard anything like this before! He looked up just in time to see a never-seen-before creature sailing through the air.

The creature twisted himself around and landed; WHUMP!

He landed feet first on the ground and then continued to slide down the slope.

Sunny Bunny had never seen anything so wonderful before. Why that was exactly what he was wishing he could do in this snowy world! Maybe if he sat in this very spot he would see it again!

Meanwhile, Jonathan, who just happened to be the snowboarder Sunny had just sighted, was feeling great about that last jump and perfect landing! He was definitely going to try that again! One quick slide and he was in line and ready to go up the lift. All Jonathan could think about was taking that terrific jump again!
At the same time, Sunny was still waiting to see if "Whatever-it-was" was coming back.

Then he heard it!...the whoop, the laugh and ... There he was!...Airborn... and coming down fast, very fast! Before either knew what was happening, Jonathan landed scooping the startled bunny right off his feet! Together the two of them were streaking down the mountainside!

"Oh, such fun, such speed, such height!", thought Sunny, hanging on for all he was worth to Jonathan's leg! Jonathan, so utterly shocked by the ordeal, lost his balance and tumbled down the hill! Worried he may have hurt the bunny, Jonathan righted himself on his board and slid over to the bunny.

To his amazement the bunny jumped back onto the board ready to go again!

Together the two of them rode the board carefully down the mountain.

As they approached the bottom of the hill, Jonathan cruised to a stop, lifted his goggles and removed his pack. Still, the bunny remained on the board. Taking an apple from his pack, Jonathan held it out to Sunny. Sunny eagerly took the apple and ran to the nearest burrow (which just happened to be Jonathan's pack). Sunny enjoyed the apple even more than rose hips and felt quite comfortable in the pack.

He had no intentions of leaving!

After a time, Jonathan gently picked up the pack and strapped it onto his back, fully expecting the bunny to leap out. He did not! So up the lift they went, Sunny Bunny comfortably riding in the pack.

At the top of the mountain Jonathan took off his back pack and tried to coax Sunny out.

Once Sunny saw the snowboard he ran out and hopped right on! Together the boy and the hare took a careful ride down the slopes. Sunny loved it!

After another run Sunny began to worry that his Mom might be missing him so he hurried back to his den.

Jonathan headed straight to his favorite shop, RED SHRED'S BIKE AND BOARD SHED, where he bought an old, used skateboard deck and a few odds and ends that might be useful for what he was about to do.

That evening Jonathan worked to make a mini-sized snowboard, complete with bindings, for the one and only snowboarding bunny!

That night Jonathan could hardly sleep, wondering what tomorrow might bring! Not too far away Sunny Bunny was nestled in his cozy den in the woods dreaming of cruising down the mountain slope with the wind whistling past his ears.

Just as Jonathan anticipated, the next morning Sunny Bunny was waiting by the jump for another adventure in snowboarding. What Sunny Bunny wasn't expecting was a board of his very own to ride! And the fit was perfect! With a flex of his legs and a small shove from Jonathan, Sunny Bunny was away!

That first run on his own was everything he imagined it would be. The wind was whistling past his ears, filling his nostrils and wildly ruffling his fur. At the bottom of the hill Jonathan took off his pack and Sunny knowingly climbed in. At the top of the lift out came the board and on jumped Sunny! This time Jonathan led the way, taking him over a few small jumps. Sunny's big feet held firm to the board.

Jonathan was certain he saw Sunny's eyes light up with delight as he soared through the air and landed squarely on the transition. Sunny was really beginning to get the hang of turning the board this way and that by a slight twist of his body and transferring his weight from one big foot to the other. He felt comfortable following in Jonathan's path!

It was about the fourth run down the mountain that Sunny had his first fall. The jump came too fast and too high. Sunny was trying too hard to do the moves he made last Fall, while throwing Wylee Fox off his scent. He landed on his back, knocking the wind out of himself. But the worst thing of all was seeing his snowboard fly through the air and slide on its own down the mountain faster than he could ever catch it!

Jonathan, seeing Sunny Bunny wasn't hurt, went chasing after the board and soon returned with it! Sunny knew that he had a friend for life now. This boy would always be special to him.

It was a friendship that would continue long after the snow melted and the ground started sprouting green grass and flowers.

Oh yes, if you are ever strolling through the forest and happen to see a mini-sized snowboard partially hidden under a log in the grass; please don't touch it or move it! It is a very special piece of equipment for a very unusual snowshoe hare called Sunny Bunny!

...About Snowshoe Hares

Snowshoe Hares live in the northern forests of Canada and the United States. They do not hibernate but stay active during the Winter. Their wide feet act like snowshoes, enabling them to get around on the snow.

The babies are born in dens, fully furred with open eyes. They are able to hop around soon after birth.

Hares have long strong hind legs. In the Summer months the hares fur is different shades of brown and gray, but they turn mostly white in the Winter.

Hares are vegetarian, eating plants and grass. In Winter they have to eat the twigs and bark above the snow.

Meet and learn about another character from the Huckleberry Hollow Series.

Meet Harry Bear

in

Huckleberry Tea